CONTENTS

Walk		Start GR	Distance	Page
•	Contents			1
•	Introduction			3
1	Chelmsley Wood/Kingshurst			
	- River Cole westwards	Various	¾ to 12 miles	8
2	Bickenhill Circle	4184 2829	5¼ miles	11
3	Earlswood - Wythall Heath	4111 2739	6¼ miles	14
4	Brueton Park - Grand Union Canal	4163 2790	4 miles	17
5	Meriden - Allesley	4252 2821	5½ miles	19
6	Monkspath - Cheswick Green	4138 2770	6 or 6½ miles	21
7	Temple Balsall - Barston			
	- Balsall Street	4208 2761	2, 3¾ or 5½ miles	24
•	Location Map			26
8	Hockley Heath - Packwood	4153 2728	4½ or 6 miles	30
9	Chadwick End - Grand Union Canal	4206 2731	5½ or 8 miles	33
10	Catherine de Barnes			
	- Hampton in Arden - Barston	4181 2805	7½ miles	37
11	Solihull Lodge			
	- Stratford upon Avon Canal	4103 2785	3¾ miles	40
12	Balsall Street - Fen End	4224 2771	3½ or 5½ miles	42
•	Castle Bromwich Festival Way 1994	4154 2899	5 miles	45
•	Meer End - Kenilworth Castle	4244 2744	6 miles	48
•	Other publications			50
•	Useful addresses and contacts			51
•	The Country Code			52

The sketch maps are reproduced from the Ordnance Survey mapping with the permission of the Controller of HMSO under Licence No. LA 076333

~ Introduction ~

This second booklet is a revised compilation of 12 more circular walks, mostly on Public Rights of Way in and around Solihull, which were previously published in 1995. Also included is an urban walk, Castle Bromwich's Festival Way, which was the local Ramblers' Association's contribution to the Festival Week in March 1994 which celebrated 100 years of Castle Bromwich Parish Council and a new walk from Meer End to Kenilworth Castle.

At the time of going to press, the routes described were the Public Right of Way routes, except where the text says otherwise. It may be that, in time, diversions will alter some routes. When diversions are confirmed, there will be sufficient waymarker arrows displayed to identify the new route to be walked. It is also hoped that the enjoyment of the walks will not be marred when changes occur on the ground and the text becomes out of date.

Parking in the countryside can lead to problems since off-road parking facilities are often not available. With this in mind, when the walks were first introduced in 1994 in leaflet form, many of the walks were started from public houses where permission had been given for the use of their car parks. However, since then some ownership and management changes have taken place - if public house car parking facilities are used, please obtain permission.

~ Public Rights of Way ~

Public Rights of Way are Highways and this booklet makes use of those ways in the countryside. In Solihull they are either Public Footpaths (124 miles/200km) for walkers only or Public Bridleways (7 miles/11km) open to walkers, cyclists and horse riders. Their position and status are recorded on the Definitive Map and Statement of Public Rights of Way which is held in the Environment Services Department. They are also recorded on Ordnance Survey maps at the scales of 1:25000 and 1:50000. However, as the network is constantly changing, mostly due to legal orders of creation, diversion or extinguishment, the up-to-date position of any right of way is best checked on the working copy of the Definitive Map in the Environment Services Department.

Although many Public Rights of Way were recorded in the Inclosure Awards of the late 18th century (held at Warwick County Record Office), in modern times the recording of Public Rights of Way was required under the National Parks and Access to the Countryside Act of 1949. Definitive maps were published in 1961 for those parts of the present Metropolitan Borough, then being Solihull Borough (the rural area only) and the Rural District of Meriden - this explains the prefixes to the path numbers of SL and M. A revision of these maps, long overdue and including paths in the previous excluded built-up area of Solihull (now prefixed U), was published in 1993. This new revision consisted of 20 No sheets at 1:10 000 scale. Some anomalies (and errors) in the 1961 map were identified - they have been investigated and the necessary Orders required to correct them put in hand. As a result of comments received, certain corrections are required to be made to the 1993 Map and Statement. These corrections, the loss of some footpaths transferred to other Authorities under the Boundary Review of April 1994 and subsequent Confirmed Orders - will result in a Definitive Map Modification Order (now reduced to 19 sheets) hopefully being advertised in 1998. NB. there are many other urban public footpaths which have been recorded as adopted highways.

~ Maintenance and Obstruction ~

Solihull Metropolitan Borough Council, being the Highway Authority, has the responsibility, on behalf of the Public, of keeping the Definitive Map up to date and the Public Rights of Way open. There are various Acts which can be enforced by the Council to ensure this, notably The Highways Act of 1980 and The Rights of Way Act of 1990.

The Council has the sole responsibility of maintaining bridges over rivers and streams, signposting where a right of way leaves a metalled road and clearing natural surface vegetation. The Council must also ensure that the landowner maintains the stiles and the hedges adjacent to paths. Also, that the way is not obstructed by growing crops, a locked gate, certain types of bull, ploughing not reinstated, electric or barbed wire fences or misleading notices. But the walker too has responsibilities and it should always be remembered that, in most cases, the land over which the Public has the "right of way", is owned by the landowner and not the Council, nor is it Public land. The walker's responsibilities are aptly listed in the

Countryside Commission's Country Code which is given on page 52. Any problem or perceived obstruction should be reported to either the Council's Footpaths Officer, George Kenneth, on telephone number 0121 704 6429 or to the local Parish Council - many parishes have a Footpaths Committee.

~ Walks in Solihull ~

The purpose of this booklet is to whet the readers appetite by laying out circular walks on Public Rights of Way in the hope that this will give the confidence needed to broaden the reader's enjoyment of the Countryside and to plan, with the aid of the map, his or her own walks, perhaps over longer routes and over more rugged terrain - or perhaps to join one of the many active rambling groups in the Borough.

Two long distance walks pass through Solihull. The Heart of England Way, was formed in 1978, and officially opened in 1990 and is now 96 miles/155 km in length from Milford Common in Staffordshire to Bourton on the Water in Gloucestershire - some 10 miles/16km of the route being within the Borough. In 1993 the Grand Union Canal Towpath Walk was opened to celebrate the 200th anniversary of the Acts of Parliament passed to build the canal. The walk from Gas Street Basin in Birmingham to Little Venice in London is 140 miles/225 km long (9 miles/14½ km being in Solihull). 6 miles/9½ km of The Stratford-upon-Avon Canal also passes through the Borough. It should be noted that only two short sections of towpath in Solihull are also Public Rights of Way (one on each canal). The remainder are permissive paths ie. paths over which the landowner permits the Public to use. Public Rights of Way Laws do not apply, although the "visitor" has the benefit of the owner's "duty of care". The North Worcestershire Path ends near Solihull Lodge and it is hoped that there will soon be a direct link from it to The Millstream Way via Birmingham and Project Kingfisher to Chelmsley Wood. A Solihull Way is a 17/20 mile waymarked route between Earlswood Lakes and Castle Bromwich Hall Gardens.

~ Access to the Countryside ~

It is a source of some dismay that the joys of the countryside experienced on these walks are denied to a section of the community - those people with disabilities. Whilst access for the less mobile for example, has been made easier on the eastern outskirts of Knowle, there are many difficulties in creating an access and surface on Public Rights of Way which is suitable for the use of wheelchairs - not least being the matter of land ownership and land use. Where the Council owns the land eg. the larger areas of Parks or Public Open Spaces, there are usually metalled paths. However, one area that will hopefully offer some scope for those using wheelchairs is on Canal Towpaths. Here British Waterways is undertaking work to open up towpaths and the Council is pursuing a policy of improving the access.

The efforts of a group of volunteers from the Birmingham CHA Rambling Club from February 1994 has been greatly appreciated. Access has been much improved in the rural Parishes of Solihull with their work in erecting stiles, kissing gates and footbridges. Acknowledgement is also given of the help of the Kenilworth Footpath Preservation Group who have adopted some footpaths adjacent of the Borough boundary in Balsall and Berkswell Parishes.

~ Equipment ~

Those undertaking the walks are advised to: wear strong, comfortable shoes or boots and thick socks (remember Solihull means "the muddy hill"); wear loose, light layers of clothing; take a waterproof and an extra sweater; and take refreshment of some sort eg chocolate and a drink. A stick is very useful as a balancing aid and to discourage the close attentions of farm animals. The recommended map which should be used is the Ordnance Survey 1:25000 pathfinder map - four sheets (934, 935, 954 and 955) cover the Borough - look out for the new Explorer series. Although only two 1:50000 landranger maps (sheets 139 and 140) cover the Borough - the larger scale map has the advantage of showing all field boundaries which is a great help in navigation. Allow plenty of time and remember to lock your car securely when you leave it in a safe place.

~ Walk Times ~

It is always difficult to gauge the time that should be allowed to undertake a walk and, of course, this can be critical if public transport connections have to be made. There are so many variables eg the make-up of the group - old, young or all ages; the number in the party - the fitness and speed of the slowest member dictates the party's speed; whether or not stops are made to eat, take photographs, watch wildlife or take in the scenery; if climbing is involved (although this is not a problem in Solihull); the ability of the party - being countrywise, able to read a map and hopefully not get lost. The times given in this booklet should be used as a guide for a brisk pace, which may need adjustment to your own speed. It is therefore best to time yourself on a walk and ascertain your speed per mile or kilometre. As a general rule allow a minimum of 25 minutes per mile.

~ Public Conveniences ~

The smaller villages have never had this provision and many toilet blocks have been demolished because of continuing vandalism. So apart from those that can be found in the main shopping areas and some parks, there are only: Avenue Road Car Park, Dorridge; Station Road/Warwick Road, Knowle; and Main Road, Meriden opposite the Police Station.

~ And Finally ~

It is said that going for a walk in the Countryside is the most popular recreational activity - I hope that this booklet will go some small way to make it enjoyable. There are 140,000 miles of Public Rights of Way in England and Wales - so there is a lot to explore!

Note: As the 1:25000 pathfinder map does not give an explanation on how to obtain grid references (GR), the full numerical reference is given in the text ie 4245 (eastings) 2791 (northings) which is more usually expressed as SP245 791.

WALK 1

A Stroll by the River Cole from Chelmsley Wood/Kingshurst - ¾ to 12 miles

This is a linear walk from any of 3 car parks in North Solihull for however long you wish and then retrace your steps to the start point OR from either Chelmsley Wood Town Centre Car Park or either of the Babbs Mill Open Space Car Parks to Stechford Lane and returning from there by No. 55 West Midlands Travel bus.

It can be a pleasant stroll round Babbs Mill Lake of ¾ mile (1.1 km) watching birds (including great crested grebe) and the antics of youngsters learning to sail - see also Strolling in Solihull's Public Parks leaflet No. 2 OR it could be a trip into the very heart of Birmingham by walking along the Cole Valley and then following the canals - a distance of 12 miles (19 km) from Chelmsley Wood with only a few hundred yards of the route along roads.

The River Cole's source is near Hob Hill to the south of Wythall, from where it meanders for 20 miles (32 km) to join with the River Blythe and then flow into the nearby River Tame near Shustoke. It first enters Solihull at Solihull Lodge, then passes through Birmingham via Sparkhill to reappear at Kingshurst and then head for Coleshill. The River Cole Valley forms a narrow strip of almost continuous open space land through Solihull and Birmingham. A glance at an old Ordnance Survey map published around 1930 shows just how much it has changed from a rural to urban river.

The Valley shown on the sketch map from Coventry Road north and eastwards through Birmingham and the entire length in North Solihull - 7 miles in total - is cared for by Project Kingfisher whose Rangers run a full programme of events throughout the year. For information contact them on 0121 749 3131 or pick up a leaflet at your Tourist Information Centre.

To help you to plan your walk here are the main features on the walk:

Miles	Km		
0	0	Chelmsley Wood Town Centre Car Park	GR 4178 2871
½	1.0	Babbs Mill Car Park (Fordbridge Road)	GR 4174 2879
1¼	2.0	Babbs Mill Car Park (Youth Afloat)	GR 4164 2878
2½	4.0	Lea Ford Road	
3	5.0	Cole Hall Lane	
4½	7.3	Stechford Lane/Station Road	
7	11.0	Coventry Road	
12	19.0	Birmingham Town Centre	

NB: From Chelmsley Wood Town Centre cross over Chelmsley Road and enter Meriden Park (see also Strolling in Solihull's Public Parks leaflet No. 4), crossing over the bridge at the end of the lake and following the south side of the River Cole to Cooks Lane.

In Babbs Mill Park it is best to follow the river's north side until the lake, after which either side is suitable. Beyond the lake, the river's north side should be followed.

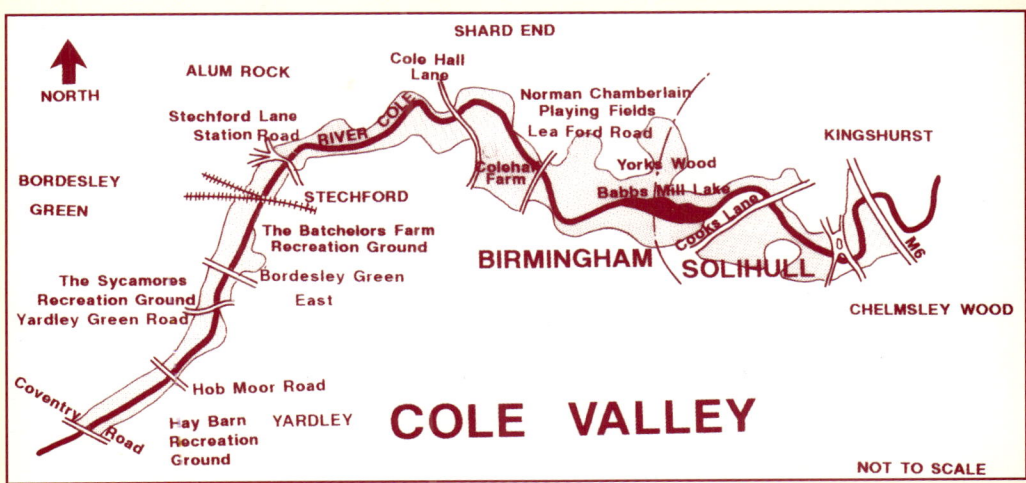

Yorks Wood Local Nature Reserve

There is evidence of a wood being here for a very long time and the 25 acre site remains as a valuable haven for wildlife in the heart of a built-up area. The wood and the land to the west was used as a camping ground by the Scout Association from the 1920's until the 1970's. When the Scouts moved to Blackwell Court near Bromsgrove, the wood was purchased by Solihull Council to become a nature reserve. Only the site of the bonfire hollow remains, with its memories of many a rousing chorus.

The wood is mostly oak with plenty of hazel and birch. Over the years many other species have been planted including scots pine and larch and among the more obscure, two false acacia or locust trees. The wood provides a home for a wealth of wildlife and many birds live in its branches. The carpet of bluebells in May is worth a visit. Enter into the wood from the end of Fordbridge Road next to The Lakeside Club and follow the meandering paths back to the start point.

South Barn, Grange Farm

WALK 2

Bickenhill Circle - 5¾ miles

This walk is centred on the hamlet of Bickenhill. The name is thought to be derived from Bica's Hill, Bica being a leader of the earliest Saxon settlement. The settlement is now a Conservation Area including several buildings of architectural and historic merit. St. Peter's Church is an early example of Norman architecture, dating from 1140.

A minimum of 2¾ hours should be allowed to complete the walk of approximately 5¾ miles (9km) over Public Rights of Way. As Catherine de Barnes Lane cuts through the walk - it can, if required, be used to split the walk into two shorter walks.

The starting point is "The Clock" P.H. situated on the westbound carriageway of the A45 Coventry Road, or accessed from the end of Clock Lane off Catherine de Barnes Lane. Those with cars please obtain permission to use the rear Public House car park GR 4184 2829.

From the car park proceed southwards down Clock Lane to meet Catherine de Barnes Lane and then cross over to follow St. Peter's Lane into Bickenhill. Where this road turns sharp right, carry straight on, on the track signposted Hazel Farm. Continue on the track past the farm. At it's end follow the hedge (on the left) for a short distance and then cross over to the stile at the gate. The next field is somewhat large, featureless and often planted, but a usually well worn path takes you on a route between a clump of trees surrounding a pond (on the right) and the pylon (on the left). At the brow of the hill, head for the gate which leads to a bridge over the M42. Follow the track which turns right down to the farm. Look out for and cross the stile (about 120 paces from track corner) on the left and bear right to the stile at the far corner of the orchard. From there follow a row of stiles to Shadowbrook Lane. Turn right along the road, crossing over the M42 and immediately turn left over the crash barrier steps. At the second stile, cross over and turn right to follow the hedge, over a number of stiles at gates, to Catherine de Barnes Lane. Turn right and after the house opposite, named "Four Winds," cross the road to the stile. Follow the boundary of "Four Winds" to the corner and turn right to head for the stile to the left of the gate which itself is to the left of the rugby posts. These "Rugby Posts" are in fact Gaelic Football posts belonging to Warwickshire Gaelic Athletic Association.

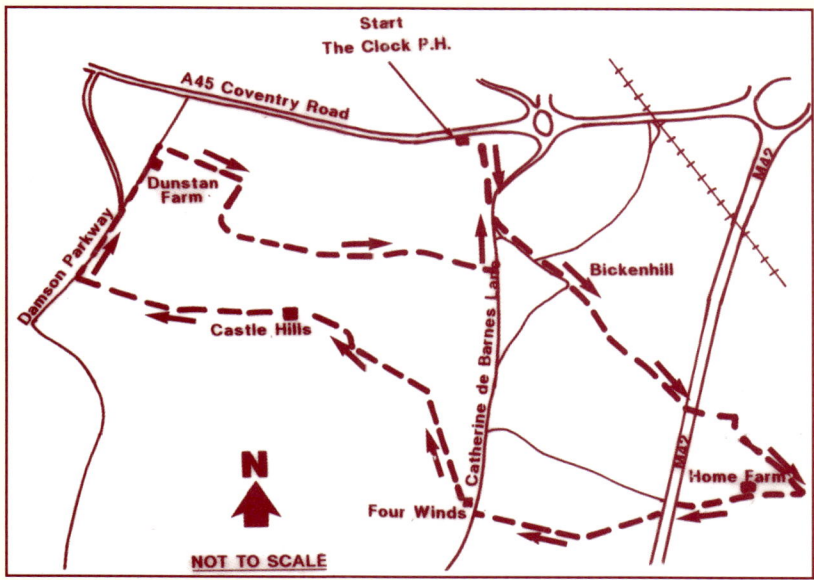

Follow the hedge on the right past the ground, until a small footbridge is seen, below on the right, just beyond the Club's Pavilion. Turn left across the field in the direction of the distant farm buildings surrounded by trees and look out for the steps which lead down to a footbridge and stile. Bear right, diagonally across the next field, in the direction of the farm buildings (if visible). As you get closer to the farm, an assortment of corrugated iron surrounding a tipped area are seen - there is a stile by the oak tree here. Continue around the tipped area - Castle Hills Farm then comes into view - head for the stile to the right of the barn. Go around to the right hand side of the farm buildings and follow the track down to the footbridge. Cross over and follow the hedge on the left to a stile where the path enters a narrow enclosed section between the hedge and the fence. Follow the path to Damson Parkway. Turn right along Damson Parkway and then right into Old Damson Lane. Go past Dunstan Farm and The Dirt Buggy Racing Centre, take the stile on the right. Follow the hedge on the left past Birmingham Civil Service Sports Ground to a footbridge. Turn right along the bottom of the bank of tipped material. Follow the waymarkers and at the second manhole, go up the now less steep bank to the field. With the hedge on the right, follow the fields round to the track. Turn right, and where the track turns right, go straight ahead to the stile passing a ruined building. Head for the church spire and look out for the waymarkers which point to a small footbridge. Cross the stile and another footbridge and follow the track, passing Birmingham Exiles Rugby Ground, to Catherine de Barnes Lane. Turn left and back down Clock Lane to the car park.

See also Walk 6 in booklet 1 which abuts this walk.

TEN COMMANDMENTS OF MOUNTAINEERING

(and equally appropriate to Rambling)

1. *Thou shalt prepare thoroughly before starting.*
2. *Thou shalt set out early.*
3. *Thou shalt set out properly equipped.*
4. *Thou shalt choose thy company with care.*
5. *Thou shalt not destroy anything that is thy neighbour's.*
6. *Thou shalt often keep silence to hear the mountain speak.*
7. *Thou shalt leave no sign of thy passing.*
8. *Thou shalt remember others in their strength or weakness.*
9. *Thou shalt bend to the weather and be strong.*
10. *Thou shalt be humble and praise God.*

Engine House, Earlswood Lakes

WALK 3

Earlswood - Wythall Heath - 6¼ miles

This walk starts from Tanworth-in-Arden Parish Council's Recreation Ground car park (GR 4111 2739) between Nos 55 and 65 Malt House Lane in Earlswood. Look out for the telephone box and the "toilets" signpost at the entrance. Rail travellers can pick up the walk from either The Lakes or Earlswood railway stations. Buses to the start point are infrequent on week days and non existent at weekends!

The walk is approximately 6¼ miles (10 km) long and takes in parts of the Counties of Warwickshire and Worcestershire. It will take a minimum of 2¾ hours to complete.

Go down to the bottom corner of the car park, through the gate (we will return on the path to the left) and follow the causeway over the reservoir - formed in 1810 to feed the adjacent Stratford-upon-Avon Canal. As you cross over - see how many species of wildfowl you can spot on the water. After the remains of the boathouse on the right, cross over the footbridge on the left and enter into Solihull. Follow the path up to the road and turn left. Just before Field Cottage cross the stile on the right and follow the field edge on the left to another stile. Cross diagonally over to the gap in the left hand hedge line and enter the adjacent field. Turn right, make for the gate by the battery house and continue to Rumbush Lane. Turn left and go along the road past Fulford Hall Road and Wood Lane. After Kidpile Farm turn right (a slight deviation from the Definitive Map) through the gap in the hedge and follow the field edge round to the signpost which directs you to two stiles. Follow the left hand hedge, crossing over two more stiles. From the last stile, bear right towards the railway underbridge - cross the River Cole, the boundary of Solihull, and at the stile gain access to a path between hedges alongside the golf course.

Turn left at the road and continue along Station Road for approximately 600 metres. Opposite the school, take the footpath on the left alongside the hedge on the right with deer farm beyond to another road. Turn left and after approximately 170 metres go through the gate in the ranch-style fencing on the right - the section to the next road is a bridleway. Cross over the road on to the path signposted Forshaw Heath. Where the two drives separate, turn right at the signpost and follow the path down to the two stiles. Cross over a field to a bridge and another small field to a stile. Then go up the hill on a well defined path to the gate by the road. Turn right and then first right along Forshaw Heath Road. Turn left down Juggins Lane and just before the entrance to Oak Tree Farm, turn left into the wood at the marker post. Follow the path round to the edge of the residential park and cross the footbridge. Continue beyond with a fence on the left, turn left at the second stile and left at the road. Turn right down the track at Lodge Farm.

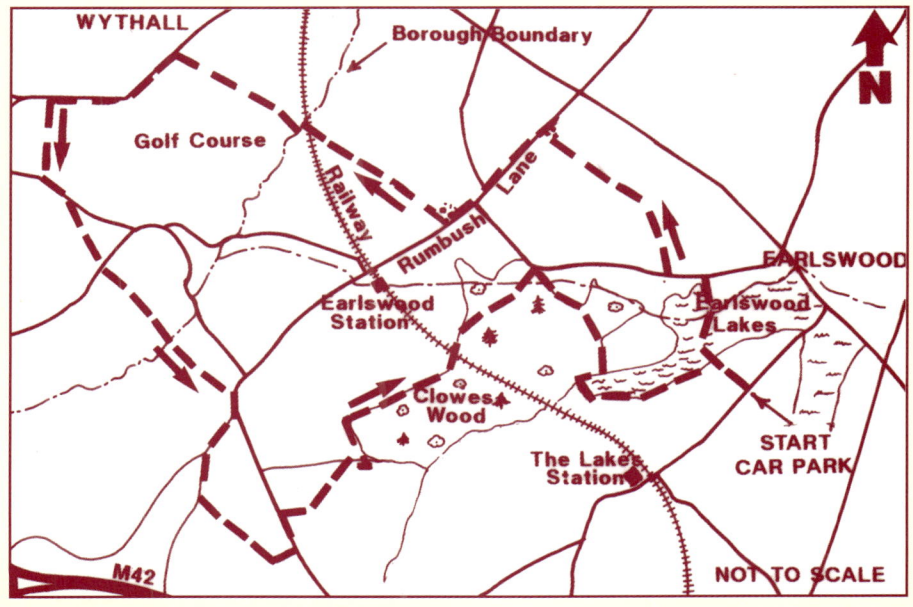

Beyond the farm buildings is a stile, from here the map shows the path going diagonally across the field to the farthest bottom corner, but, I was asked to follow the field round to the left to the stile. Cross this stile, turn right and almost immediately cross the next stile - this manoeuvre taking you into the adjacent field. Follow the hedge on the left to another stile, then go up the side of Clowes Wood and into the wood at the top corner.

Keep parallel to the wood edge (on the left) to the railway line and cross over it by the footbridge. The next section is more difficult to navigate as the wood does not give us any points to aim for! From the footbridge continue straight ahead for a short distance and then bear left to the wooden footbridge. From there keep on the path parallel to the wood's edge, until after about 90 paces the path forks - take the right hand route which leads to an area of mature beech, oak and a solitary conifer - go down the hill past some cut down trees and a footbridge should come into view. Beyond the bridge a well worn path leads to a small car park. Don't go through the kissing gate, but, either go into the camping field and follow the wood's edge to the gap in the hedge just before the gateway, passing a boundary stone, to the log cabin OR keep in the wood and parallel to its edge and look for the log cabin. At the farthest fence corner and with your back to the log cabin, go down the well defined straight path. At the path junction turn left - this leads to a footbridge at the reservoir. Turn right and follow the path on the waters edge back to the car park.

The sketch shows the red brick 19th Century Engine House (Pumping Station) in Valley Road - a grade 2 listed building.

St. Alphege Church

WALK 4

Brueton Park - Grand Union Canal - 4 miles

This walk starts from Brueton Park car park situated on the "Old" Warwick Road but it can also be started from the very heart of Solihull. From St Alphege Church go down New Road and take Park Road into Malvern Park where the route can be picked up at Boehm's statue.

The walk is approximately 4 miles (6½ km) long and will take a minimum of 80 minutes to complete. Toilet facilities are available in Brueton Park - see also Strolling in Solihull's Public Parks leaflet 5. The first half of this walk follows the more rural route of A Solihull Way

Go back out of the car park (Grid Reference 4163 2790) and turn right up "Old" Warwick Road. Turn left down Barston Lane to its end and continue on the tarmac path beyond, up to the by-pass. Cross over the dual carriageway where visibility is clear, to the sign post opposite. Follow the path, initially tarmaced, down to the gate and continue between fences and parallel to the M42. At the next gate follow the motorway fence to a tarmac footpath which then becomes a road - the other end of Barston Lane. Cross over the canal bridge and immediately take the path down to the towpath at Henwood Wharf. Proceed northwards along the Grand Union Canal towpath. Don't be alarmed if you meet cyclists on the towpath - it is British Waterways' policy to promote cycling. Leave the towpath at the next bridge, crossing over it and then turning immediately left around British Waterways' gate.

Follow the galvanised steel palisade fence round to the stile at the corner. From here a well defined path goes through the middle of a small field to another stile. Then follow the hedge, on the right, over two stiles where the Esso pipeline crosses, to the stile by the gate at Ravenshaw Lane. Almost opposite is another stile, cross over it and head for the far right hand corner of the field. A gate leads to a path between the wood and Berry Hall Farm. After the next stile, where access is gained to a field - follow the hedge on the left to pick up a gravel path laid some years ago by the Ramblers' Association.

At the second stile another field opens out and we make for the top right hand corner, to follow the hedge, on the right, through three kissing gates to the by-pass. Go over the by-pass, cross Avenbury Drive and after crossing Marsh Lane, go up Oakley Wood Drive. At No.19 take the tarmac path to Hampton Lane. Turn left here, cross Warwick Road at the traffic lights, turn right and then bear left down New Road.

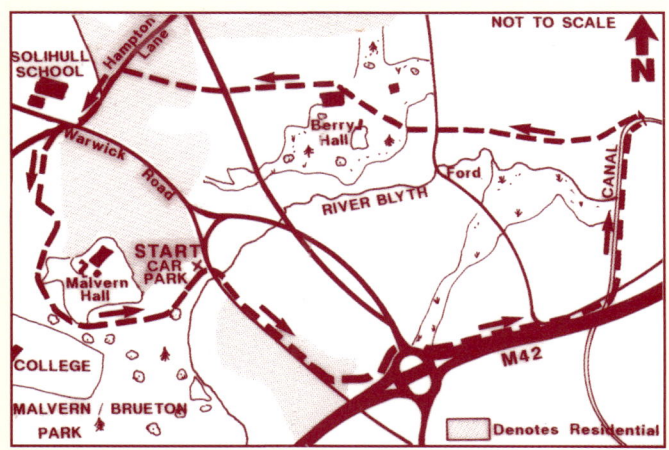

Turn left into Malvern Park through the wrought iron gates - compare these traditional gates with those at the large house next to Old Silhillians Sports Ground on the south side of the A41/M42 interchange. (The design of these award-winning gates is in the form of a floral extraviganza depicting an all-year round garden with forged evergreen leaves for winter, daffodils for spring, roses and wild lilies for summer, vines and grapes for autumn). Follow the path, past the children's play area, to Boehm's imposing statue of horse and horse tamer. Continue around the park's edge with the tennis courts on the far right and round the back of the listed Malvern Hall, now St Martin's School, and into Brueton Park. If you wish, take in the wildlife reservation with its exotic birds, rabbits, guinea pigs and hidden pond or visit the larger open pond with its resident geese/duck population - before getting back to the car park. These two interlinked parks, totalling some 135 acres, form Solihull's most beautiful and unspoilt park. This walk can be extended by adding on Walk 10 in this booklet.

Meriden Cross

WALK 5

Meriden - Allesley - 5½ miles

This walk starts from Old Road adjacent to "The Queen's Head" on the eastern outskirts of Meriden. Either park in the road or obtain permission to use the Public House car park (GR 4252 2821). The walk is approximately 5½ miles (8¾ km) long and takes in part of the City of Coventry District's area where a major access initiative has produced excellent waymarking and where kissing gates are the norm. Part of the route in Solihull follows a bridleway where walkers can expect to meet horse riders and cyclists. Public toilets are available in Meriden's Main Road, opposite the Police Station. For information about Meriden - see Doreen Agutter's booklet 'Meriden Centre of England'

With your back to the Queen's Head turn left and follow Eaves Green Lane for approximately 220 yards (200m) to the track on the right alongside the house named Camelot. Go up the track to its end then bear slightly left across the field to the gateway. Follow the hedge on the left through the gateway (on left - Diversion Order confirmed 1997) to the next gate adjacent to the lane. Stay in the field and follow the roadside hedge to the stile at the corner near the by-pass. Turn right under the by-pass and continue beyond where Lodge Green Lane joins from the left to the bend in Showell Lane at the waterworks - this road is narrow, so take care. Turn left up the bridleway - large boulders at the entrance. Continue along the bridleway to its end at Harvest Hill Lane, turn left and almost immediately go through the kissing gate on the right. Follow the fence down to the next kissing gate at Pickford Brook - the Borough boundary. Keep the hedge on the right until it comes to a corner cross over to the hedge corner in front of the house and then turn right to the kissing gate (the beware of bull sign is always there and should be treated as advisory). From here, cross the next field to the kissing gate to the right of the farm buildings. A well waymarked path follows the hedge line beyond, with Coventry's skyline in the distance - to a lane. Turn left and then at the marker post go down the side of the house named Dovedale. The well waymarked route continues in the three fields beyond and then goes to the left of Harvest Hill Farm where a narrow section leads to Oak Lane. Turn right and at the marker post take the path round the other side of the farm.

The hedge is followed, first on the right and then at the second kissing gate, on the left - down to Pickford Brook. Follow the hedge on the right beyond to the gate, then go due west up the rise towards the manhole with the brick surround and then in the direction of the house on the skyline. As we gain height, we see a gateway, our next objective - but, first we go down to cross the drain at the culvert.

From the gate contour round the hill towards the copse in the distant foreground and keeping roughly parallel with the field boundary on the left, cross the stile and turn left up the track past Alspath Hall up to Showell Lane. Turn left and at the roundabout turn right. Continue down Meriden Hill and then take Old Road back to the start.

See walks 7 and 10 in booklet 1 for further walks starting from the Queens Head.

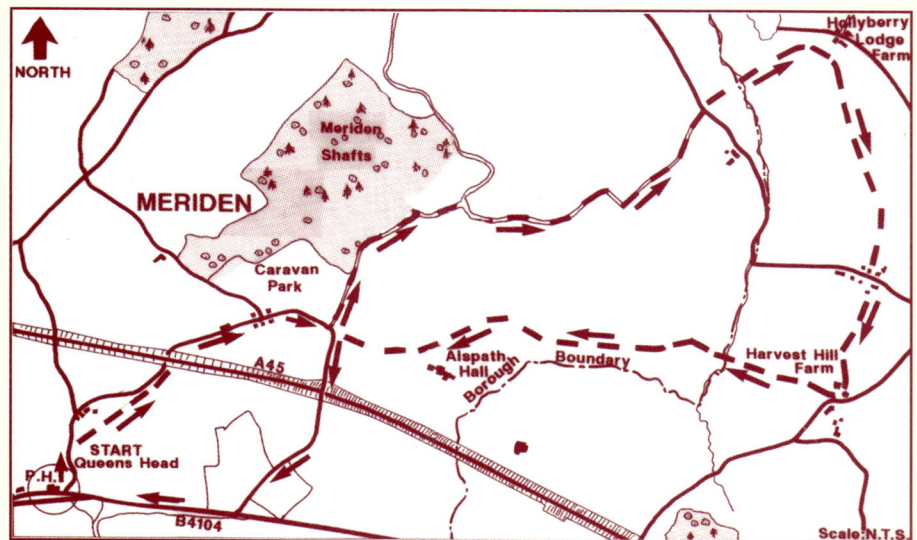

Monkspath Hall (re-built)

WALK 6

Monkspath - Cheswick Green - 6 or 6½ miles

This walk starts from the car park at Hillfield Park (GR 4138 2770) - see also Strolling in Solihull's Parks leaflet No. 9 - just off Monkspath Hall Road near to the junction with Thornton Road. The walk is over public footpaths mostly in Hockley Heath Parish. Sections of this walk follow the direct and more rural routes of A Solihull Way.

The walk is approximately 6½ miles (10½ km) long or a shorter route of 6 miles (9½ km). The longer route will take a minimum of 2¼ hours to complete.

From the car park, cross over Monkspath Hall Road and turn left along the footway. Turn right into Hay Lane and after No.64, turn left down the Monkspath. Cross over Frankholmes Drive and carry straight on. After the entrance to Rowthorn Drive, continue to the fence at housing and turn right, taking the path parallel to the back of the housing and continuing beyond past Tesco and Notcutts to the Stratford Road. Turn left over the M42 and continue on the Henley Road (A3400) past Gate Lane. Cross over after No.1779 to the stile and follow the nursery's boundary hedge to the corner (a deviation here from the Definitive Map). From here bear left to the oak tree (near mast) at the far corner of the field, adjacent to the M42. Follow the motorway fence to the bridge. Cross the bridge and turn left on the track down to the stile in the fence - a business park development is proposed here. Follow the path, cross the stile, keep to the left of the farm building, pass to the front of Sidenhales Farm (demolished by fire 1997 and pick up the path to the right of the next farm building which leads to another stile. Keep on the track beyond until just after the edge of the cultivation. Where the hedge and track turn left - we bear right through an area of scattered gorse to where there are two stiles linked by a footbridge. Follow the hedge on the left to the field corner. Turn left along the drive and at Illshaw Heath Road turn right.

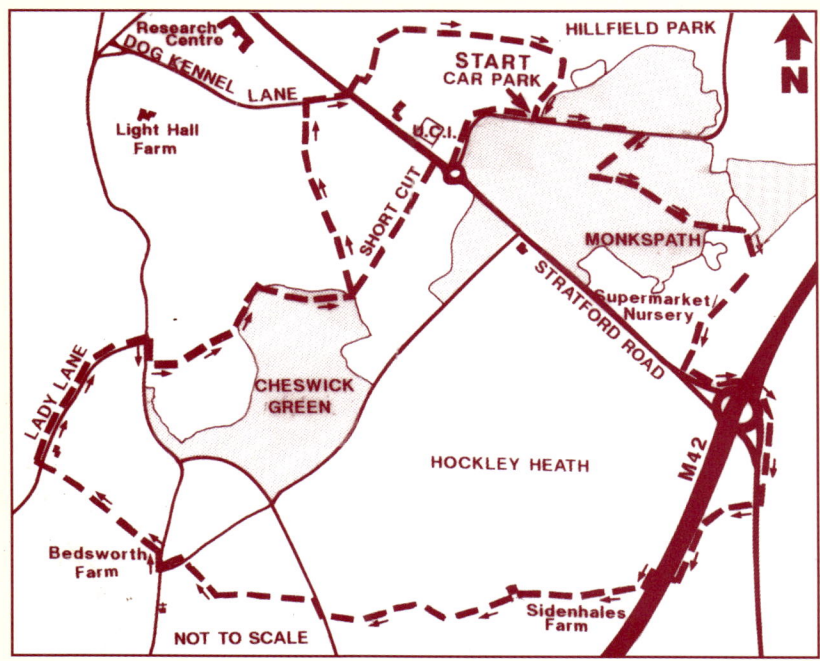

About 100 paces along the road, take the path on the left at the gate. Cross the field towards the lime tree to the right of the distant spire. Go round the edge of the wooded hollow (on the right), over the bridge and make for the stile. From here follow the line of occasional trees (and marker posts) bearing right towards the farmhouse at Vicarage Road. Turn left and then right at Salter Street. At the second gate on the left, opposite the farm buildings, cross the stile and follow the hedge on the left. After the next stile by the gate - the fence/hedge is now on the right and is followed to Lady Lane. Turn right at this road - take care as the road is narrow - pass Braggs Farm Lane and at the T road junction (Tanworth Road) turn right. After the cottage (No.527) cross the stile and follow the hedge on the left to Cheswick Green. Follow the path round the perimeter of the housing and then the tarmac path between Nos.60 and 45 Snowshill Drive. Continue on the footway towards the pylon and the road beyond. At the road junction bear left along Boscobel Road and then left at the next road also signposted Boscobel

Road. (If you continue straight on here you will come to The Mount, off Longleat Drive. The Mount was a medieval moated site. It was descheduled as an Ancient Monument when it was partly levelled in the 1970's for house building. What remains is a substantial historic earthwork giving a good wildlife habitat).

At the end of the cul-de-sac go round to the right of the garages. [From here, to avoid a section which is heavily wooded and enclosed, which may be intimidating to some walkers and to shorten the walk by ½ mile (1 km) - see the end of the text]. Continue along the back of the garages to a stile. Follow the hedge on the right in the first field and then on the left beyond to Dog Kennel Lane. Turn right, cross over and take the old road. Note the Victorian pillar box on the right - built by Smith and Hawkes at their Eagle Foundry in Birmingham - now a listed structure. Pass by Prophet's Garage, cross Stratford Road and enter Madams Hill Public Open Space on the tarmac path at the side of the end house - this is the start of the heavily wooded section previously mentioned. At the path junction turn right, under the pylon line, following the edge of the industrial estate and then underneath Highlands Road. From here a well-defined path between the pylon line and the stream leads into Hillfield Park. At the tarmac path turn right (turning left will take you round the pond) and at the Y-junction of paths, bear right back to the car park.

A longer walk can be made by adding on walk 4 in booklet 1.

FOR THE SHORTER ROUTE: after passing the side of the garages, take the stile in the hedge beyond and follow the hedge on the left to the Stratford Road. Cross over the dual carriageway and follow Monkspath Hall Road back to the car park.

The Almshouses and The Master's House, Temple Balsall

WALK 7

Temple Balsall - Barston - Balsall Street - 2, 3¾ or 5½ miles

This walk starts at Temple Balsall on the B4101 road between Knowle and Balsall Common. Cars can be parked in the visitor's car park of the Hospital of Lady Katherine Leveson, opposite the school, just south of the B4101 on Fen End Road West (Grid Reference 4208 2761).

A choice of three walks are available:

Walk 1 is approximately 2 miles   (3 km)
Walk 2 is approximately 3¾ miles   (6 km)
Walk 3 is approximately 5½ miles   (9 km)

Temple Balsall was founded by the Crusading Knights Templar in the 12th Century. These soldier monks were disbanded in the 14th Century and were succeeded by the Knights Hospitallers who were in turn disbanded by Henry VIII. The Manor was given by Queen Elizabeth to Robert Dudley, Earl of Leicester and was inherited by his grand-daughters - one of whom being Lady Katherine Leveson who founded the almshouses and school. St Mary's Church dates from the 14th Century and was restored in 1670 and again in the 1840's. Teas are available in the courtyard every Saturday, Sunday and Bank Holiday between 2.30 pm and 5 pm from Easter Saturday to the end of September.

Barston has some fine historic listed buildings in the Conservation Area around the Church of St Swithin which was built in 1721 on the site of a medieval church.

stile by the gate. Follow the hedge on the left and after the next gate, bear right round a wooded wet area to the footbridge over the River Blythe. At the stile on the left, turn right along the field edge to the corner. Cross the stile and turn left through a narrow section which leads to a track, turn right and at Barston Lane, turn left. At the foot of the hill turn right at the gateway, bear left to cross the small stream and immediately turn right into the field. Follow the stream until the field narrows - cross over to the hedge and follow it up to the corner adjacent to Wootton Lane. Continue round the field boundary past the gas pipeline compound to the stile at the next hedge corner. Continue to the next hedge junction, don't cross the stile - but turn right on The Heart of England Way, around the field boundary and down to a stile (slight deviation from the definitive route), footbridge and another stile beyond. From there, follow the hedge on the right to Balsall Street.

Turn left and just before the grade 2 listed "Ye Olde Saracen's Head", turn right down Magpie Lane. Just past the first house, cross the stile on the right. Follow the fence on the left round to the hedge and continue along the field edge to Magpie Lane. Turn left and cross the stile on the right some 80 paces along the lane. Follow the hedge, on "The Knight's Way", round the wooded wet area to its corner and head across the field to the footbridge. Cross over the narrow field to a stile and follow the hedge on the left. After passing under the pylon line, four hedges and four footpaths meet at the corner - here Walk 2 is joined from the right and The Heart of England Way turns left. We continue on the same line, but, with the hedge now on the right, to Fen End Road West. Turn right along the road to the car park.

For further options, see walks 10 and 12 in this booklet and walks 1 and 5 in booklet 2 - all abut this walk.

Please Shut the Gate

Be ye man or be ye woman

Be ye going or be ye coming

Be ye sharp or be ye late

Be ye sure to shut the gate

Packwood House

WALK 8

Hockley Heath - Packwood - 4½ or 6 miles

This walk starts at Hockley Heath and is mostly over public footpaths in Warwickshire. The starting point is "The Nags Head" (Harvester Restaurant) situated at the junction of Stratford Road and Aylesbury Road. Please obtain permission to use their car park (GR 4153 2728).

The walk is approximately 6 miles (10 km) long and will take a minimum of 2 hours to complete. Or a shorter route of approximately 4½ miles (7½ km) can be taken.

From the start point, proceed along Stratford Road (in the direction of Stratford) crossing over to the Wharf Tavern to gain access to the Stratford upon Avon Canal via the car park. Turn left along the towpath to the second drawbridge. Turn left here, off the towpath and turn left along the road. Cross the stile on the right by the gate and continue initially through a narrow field. As the field widens follow the hedge, on the left, to the gap in the hedge. Turn right alongside the hedge (on the right) to the stile in the corner. Turn left and follow the edge of the field to a gap in the hedge (direction post), go through the gap and then turn right along the drive. Cross the road to the stile opposite, keep to the right of the scots pines and head for the marker post. Follow the fence on the right, cross over the fence by the stile and continue along the field edge to the marker post at a stile. Cross a small field to another stile and follow the wood's edge past the bungalow on the right and Pratt's Pit on the left - to the road.

30

Turn left along the road, passing the topiary garden which is said to represent the Sermon on the Mount, to Packwood House. Packwood House is Tudor in period and displays furniture, paintings and tapestries. It is opened by the National Trust from April to the end of September between 2-6 on Wednesdays to Sundays (inclusive) and Bank Holiday Mondays (but closed Good Friday) and in October between 12.30 - 4.30 on Wednesdays to Sundays (inclusive).

[FOR THE SHORTER ROUTE from here - see the end of the text] Opposite the house climb the semi-circular brick steps and proceed along the National Trust's Packwood Avenue to Chessetts Wood Road. Turn left along the road and take the track on the left to Chessetts Wood Farm - after passing the house named Spinney Close. Beyond the farm follow the track round to the left to a field - go straight ahead following the field edge round to the stile, just before the waymarker on the oak tree. Follow the fence on the right to the third gate where we bear right over two footbridges and then follow the hedge on the left to the road.

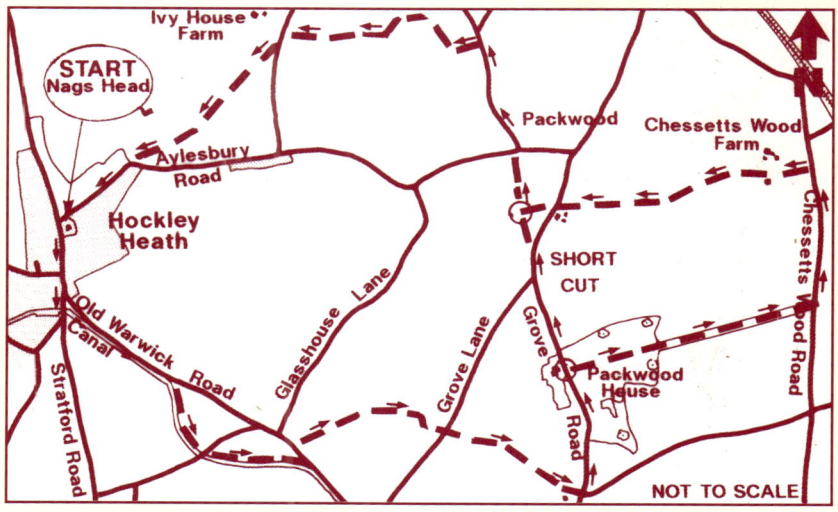

Go through the kissing gate opposite and follow the hedge on the left to a stile [WHERE THE SHORTER ROUTE IS JOINED]. Don't cross the stile but, turn right to the footbridge and re-enter Solihull. Follow the well defined path up the hill to the road. Turn right and then left up Windmill Lane. Turn left up the track after passing Packwood Moor. After Packwood Mill bear right to the gate. Follow the hedge on the right round the field to a silver birch tree (a slight deviation here from the Definitive Map route). At the hedge junction beyond, go through the gap and down to the track, where we leave Solihull and proceed up to Grove Road.

Turn left to the stile some 75 paces along the road on the right. Diagonally cross the field to the stile, don't cross it, but turn left and and from there follow the fence (on your right) to the field corner. Follow the hedge on the right beyond, to the drive (NB there is a way through the corner of the second field!) Cross the drive and go through the remains of a kissing gate, continuing to Aylesbury Road. Proceed down that road back to the start point. (NB No. 2679 Stratford Road is reputed to be the highest house number in the country?).

FOR THE SHORTER ROUTE : Continue along the road past Packwood House. After passing Grove Lane on the left, turn left into the next gateway. Bear right here - head for the electricity pole to the right of the oak tree, where a stile will come into view and the longer route is rejoined.

See also walk 11 in booklet 1 which abuts this walk.

Hill Top Heaven

There's nothing like a quiet dream high on a windy hill,

with all the world spread out below so silent and so still:

Tall grasses move and dance like Ballerinas in the breeze

and sounds-like organ music echo through the tallest trees.

Stride out-just climb a windy hill and feel your pulses stir,

fill heart and soul with happiness in real true country air,

feel clearer for the days to come when life compels your feet-

to pound the dusty pavements of a crowded city street.

Georgina Hall

Baddesley Clinton

WALK 9

Chadwick End- Grand Union Canal - 5½ or 8 miles

This walk is centred on Chadwick End, on the south eastern corner of the Borough, where a choice of two walks are available. The shorter walk (approximately 5½ miles/8¾ km) is almost entirely within Solihull, whereas the longer walk (approximately 7¾ miles/12½ km) loops into Warwickshire and passes close to the National Trust property of Baddesley Clinton.

The walk starts at Balsall Parish Council's car park (Grid Ref 4206 2731) on the north eastern side of Warwick Road in the centre of the village and adjacent to the Village Hall (look out for the Post Office sign). On football match days (presently Sundays), this car park may be full and permission to park may have to be sought at The Orange Tree public house just across the road. The longer walk will take a minimum of 3½ hours to complete.

From the Village Hall car park entrance, turn left and take the track (The Heart of England Way) on the left just before house No. 1 (waymarkers on gatepost). This leads to a cul-de-sac, where we go between Nos 55 and 57 into the garages area and then round the back of No. 55 to the field. After crossing the stile, go to the left of the hedge and continue into Priests Park Wood. Follow the path through the wood - at the path junction, turn left between two silver birches to the fields. Bear right at the site across the field towards the oak tree in the bottom corner. Beyond the gate, follow the fence/hedge through this field and the right hand boundary in the next - to the footbridge in the corner. From here we enter Warwickshire and go up the hill to a stile. The hedge beyond, on the right, is followed to a stile and a narrow field crossed to another stile. We bear left from here, cutting across the field corner in the direction of an electricity pole - from where we see the stile in the hedge beyond. After crossing the footbridge, go up the hill in the direction of the cottages, to the stile in the hedge. In the field beyond, bear right to a stile near to where the right hand fence meets the roadside hedge (a slight deviation here from the Definitive Map route).

At the road we re-enter Solihull and turn left - The Heart of England Way turns right. At the grade 2 listed Oldwich House Farm (gallery) which is reputed to be the ancestral home of the Shakespeare family - bear right along Old Green Lane. Past the ford, turn left up the track after the barn. Cross the road to the stile opposite. Follow the hedge on the left to the second stile, then follow the hedge on the right. At the road turn right past Chadwick Manor (later 19th Century in Jacobean style). At the road junction turn left. An ornamental pond is passed on the left - after it, we turn left up the drive to Park Corner and beyond between the two hedges. At the track turn right - where it turns right to the farm buildings, we proceed through the gate in front. Where a large gate leads to a house (The Dial House, grade 2), we turn left through the small gate (another slight deviation here from the Definitive Map) to Warwick Road. Turn left along the road and right - up the drive to The Black Boy. To the left of the bridge at The Black Boy, gain access to the canal towpath.

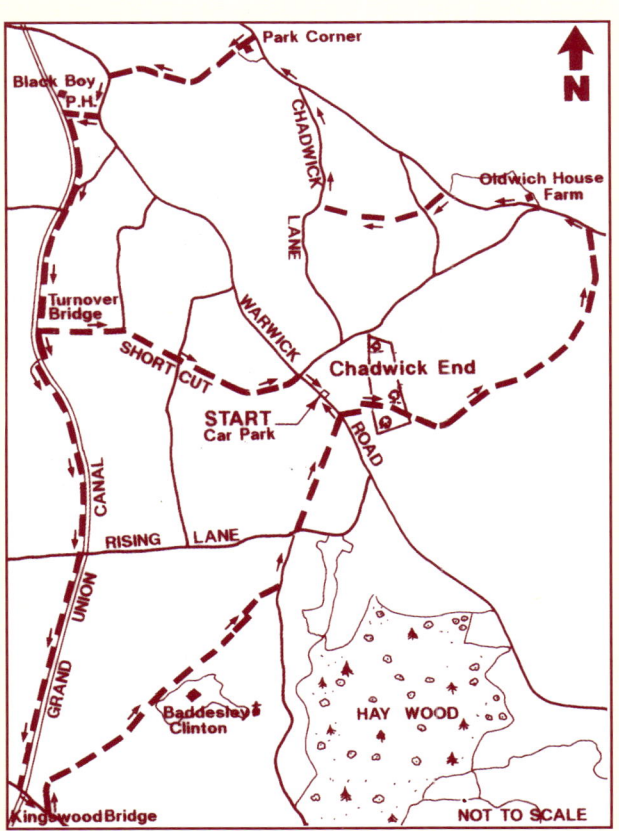

Turn left (south) along the

towpath of the Grand Union Canal, not a public right of way, but, a permissive path which will take you all the way to London. We pass the quaint grade 2 listed Haycock Farm and at Bridge 67 (Turnover Bridge) we either turn left on the shorter route (see the end of text) or right to the towpath on the opposite bank for the longer route. Shortly after this bridge we re-enter Warwickshire. At Bridge 65 (Kingswood Bridge) we go underneath and then up to the road where we turn right. Opposite the entrance to The Manor House we go up the track which leads to a large stables building to the right of which is a stile. Bear right across the field to the far corner and follow the hedge on the right in the next field to the corner. In the parkland beyond follow the fence on the right at the back of Baddesley Clinton. On the right at the fence corner is the end of the fish pond - from here cut across the corner of the field to the stile at the access drive. (Turning right here gives a short detour to St. Michael's Church and back. Note the inscription on the gravestone on the left just before the church and the display of snowdrops and daffodils in the spring.)

Turn left at the drive and after a short distance, go through the kissing gate on the right, we are now back on The Heart of England Way. The next section of path, almost entirely fenced off, leads to Hay Wood Lane where we turn left. At the junction with Rising Lane we turn right and at the footpath signpost, we turn left up the track to Convent Farm (Poor Clares Convent is further along the road). We pass through the stable yard and, keeping the hedge on our right, go through small fields until the fields narrow to a corner and a stile. From here, after passing through another field, we arrive back at Warwick Road - turning left takes us back to the car park.

FOR THE SHORTER ROUTE: Having turned left into the field at Turnover Bridge, we continue straight ahead following the field boundary to a track which leads to a road junction. Straight in front is Netherwood Lane which is followed to Warwick Road - turning right takes us back to the car park.

Baddesley Clinton: is a medieval moated Manor House - the house and gardens being open to the Public on Wednesdays - Sundays and Bank Holidays (except Good Friday) from 2-6 from early March - end of September and between 12.30 - 4.30 on Wednesdays - Sundays in October.

See also walk 12 in this booklet which abuts this walk.

Heaven on Earth

Its heaven on earth to walk alone beneath
The open skies.
To lie upon a grassy mound and watch clouds
Drifting by.
One Cloud may look just like a face, when
others form to take their place.

A panoramic changing scene,
Just like some long remembered dream.
This is a world I would not want to change,
One nature cannot rearrange.
A heaven on earth, god given and free,
For all who have the eyes to see.

So take a rucksack on your back,
Set off along a beaten track.
Happiness will guide your steps.
Though weary you may be, you'll know that
for a little while that you were truly free.

Georgina Hall

Old Timbers, Barston

WALK 10

Catherine de Barnes - Hampton-in-Arden - Barston - 7½ miles

This walk begins at Catherine de Barnes and takes in the villages of Hampton in Arden and Barston. Parking is available in Barbers Lane (GR 4181 2805) ie when proceeding out of Solihull on road B4102, turn left immediately after crossing the canal bridge and then first right after the house named Woodfield - park in the section of road up to the main road (parking may also be available at the Boat Inn, but, permission should be sought). The first section of this walk and most of the towpath, is also the route of the more rural A Solihull Way.

The walk is approximately 7½ miles (12 km) long and will take at least 2¾ hours to complete. The walk passes through two dairy farms with the inevitable consequence of all the coming and going of cows - mud! For this reason, this walk should probably be tackled after a frost or during dry spells.

The centres of Hampton-in-Arden and Barston are Conservation Areas with many listed buildings. Hampton-in-Arden was the setting for Shakespeare's play "As you like it".

At the main road turn left, continue to the roundabout and straight ahead on Solihull Road. Immediately after the farthest corner of Hampton Lane Farm, turn left over the stile at the signpost. Follow the muddy track round to the right. Cross the stile by the gate, turn immediately left and follow the hedge to the top of the field. Turn right here (ignore the stile straight ahead) and follow the hedge (on the left) to the M42 where we turn left up to Shadowbrook Lane. Turn right, passing Home farm and a number of cottages. As the road starts to go uphill and the wood on the right is past - cross the stile on the right. Follow the wood on the left to the line of iron kissing gates and then a narrow section which takes us to the High Street, Hampton-in-Arden. Turn right and pass the shops - for those with clean boots, there is a small cafe and heritage centre which displays local memorabilia from the local society - it is open daily till 2 pm except on Sundays. The road bends round the church and we turn left down Belle Vue Terrace. At the bottom of the road, turn right at the signpost, along a narrow enclosed path to a stile. Turn left and follow the hedge to the gate. Bear right into the next field and follow the hedge on the left to the footbridge.

Follow the hedge beyond (on the left) to the drive. Cross over to the small footbridge and then cross the field to the oak tree at the corner. Follow the hedge to the track and turn left - this group of houses and a farm - some are listed buildings - is named Walsal End. Walk along the track to the cattle grid at the timber-framed building. Do a U-turn here to cross the other cattle grid on the left and then turn right on the track to the front of Red Barns and The Barn. The track turns left and there is a stile on the right - from here, cross the field towards the middle of the wooded area to the right of the far left hand field corner. This leads, after passing through a small copse, to a footbridge and to another field. Cross the field to the gate and cross the next field to the hedge corner at the electricity pole - go into the next field and follow the hedge on the left to a stile from where the hedge on the right is followed to Oak Lane.

Turn right, at the main road turn left and then turn right down Hob Lane. After Blythe View House, cross the first stile on the right to follow a path, to the River Blythe. Pass to the front of the cottages and turn left along Wood Lane - you might catch sight of red deer in the first field on the right. This lane is muddy in places. Turn right at the fishing pond and at the T-junction turn left (the "Private Field" notice does not apply to us!). Follow the hedge on the right to Knowle Road. Cross to the private road opposite and follow the waymarkers past Eastcote Grange (formerly a hospital, but, now the centre of an exclusive residential area) - to the field. Turn right to the stile at the gate and bear left, round the pond to the kissing gate and follow the hedge on the left. Turn left at the gate and continue straight ahead passing the sewage works on the left, to the field corner. Cross the concrete footbridge and bear left to the footbridge over the River Blythe. Follow the edge of the pond beyond the bridge and then cross the field to the stile by the oak at the fence corner.

Follow the fence, passing in the field on the left the site of Henwood Priory founded by Benedictine Nuns c AD 1157. After passing Henwood Hall Farm (built 1824 and grade 2 listed) go along the access track. Where the access track turns right, we turn left to the field. Cross the field to the hedge corner and follow the hedge beyond. Cross the stile at the field corner and follow the fence to the Grand Union Canal. Turn left at the stile before crossing over the canal and go down the steps to the towpath. Turn right along the towpath under bridge 75. After the cricket ground bear right, off the towpath on to the tarmac drive up to Hampton Lane and then turn right, back to where the car is parked.

Numerous extensions to this walk can be tried, as walks 1 and 9 in booklet 1 and walks 2, 4 and 7 in this booklet all abut this walk.

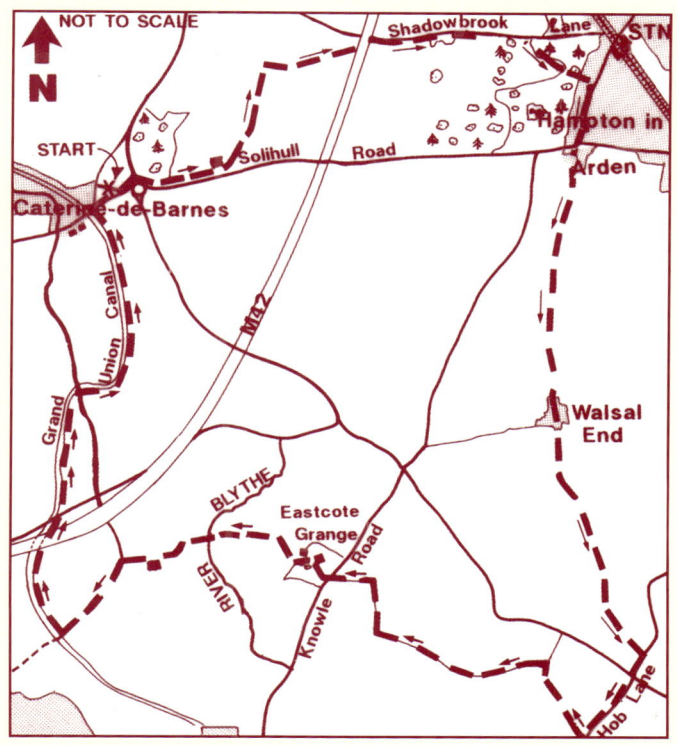

WALK 11

Solihull Lodge - Stratford-upon-Avon Canal - 3¾ miles

This walk is from Solihull Lodge to Three Maypoles, returning via the Stratford upon Avon Canal. Parts of the route are quite muddy and wellington boots are advised at certain times of the year.

The walk starts from Colebrook Recreation Ground car park (Grid Reference 4103 2785) which is situated in Green Lane next to The Play School run by The Solihull Handicapped Childrens Association. NB: the car park barrier is locked at dusk. It is approximately 3¾ miles (6km) long and will take a minimum of 1¼ hours to complete. Shirley Railway Station is close to the start - for rail and bus connections. The route is over a short section of Public Right of Way and the canal towpath is a permissive route.

From the car park turn left up Green Lane to the T-junction (Haslucks Green Road). Turn right and then left along Bills Lane. At the bend after Woods Farm (christmas trees motif on the brick wall) bear right on the track (bridleway) signposted Whitlock's End Farm. After passing the farm, take the left-hand fork in the track to the road at Three Maypoles. Turn right along Dickens Heath Road. Before the canal bridge, bear left down to the towpath. At the towpath a Public Right of Way extends for about 550 yards (500 metres) to the left, we however turn right under Bridge No 12 with Dickens Heath Village on the left.

Continuing along the towpath we cross into Hereford and Worcester after going under the railway bridge. We then pass by the built-up area of Major's Green and reach The Drawbridge Public House. At the next brick structure the canal crosses over Aqueduct Road and the River Cole - and we re-enter Solihull. At Bridge No 7, reconstructed in

1963, we leave the towpath and go up to High Street, where we turn right. After the mini roundabout junction with Aqueduct Road, the road becomes Colebrook Road and after No 131, the open space is Colebrook Recreation Ground. We turn right and follow the tarmac path beside the River Cole, over the footbridge and back to the car park beside the children's play area.

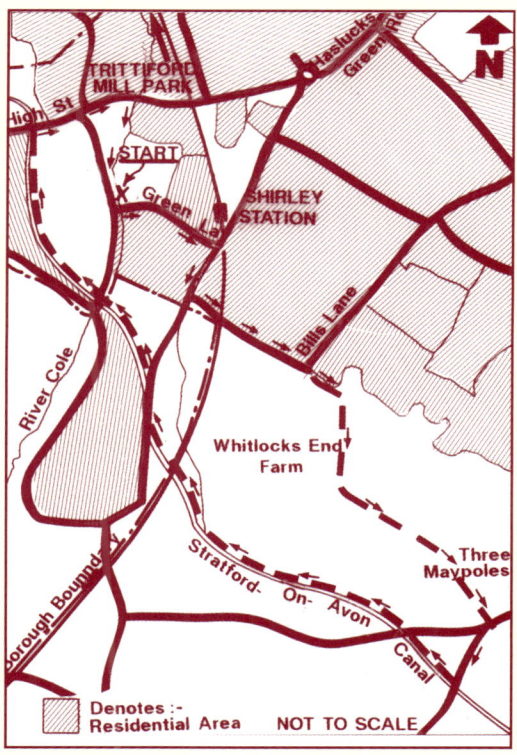

For the more adventurous, this walk can be extended by a further 2¼ miles (3½km) by taking the Public Right of Way between No 88 Colebrook Road and the railway line, to the boundary with Birmingham. The River Cole is then followed on an unofficial path to Slade Lane. Keeping to the River Cole Valley, more formal paths are followed to Scribers Lane and then into Trittiford Mill Park - where a circuit of the pond is made and the route retraced. Birmingham City Council hope eventually to extend the existing River Cole Open Space from Slade Lane to the Borough Boundary - it may be that when that happens, a link will be made with Nethercote Gardens and the path beside the railway line may then be closed?.

Ye Olde Saracen's Head

WALK 12

Balsall Street - Fen End - 3½ or 5½ miles

This walk is mostly over public footpaths in the Parish of Balsall which celebrated its centenary in 1994. Part of the route follows The Heart of England Way. Please obtain permission to park in the car park of Ye Olde Saracen's Head on Balsall Street (B4101) on the western outskirts of Balsall Common (Grid Reference 4224 2771). The walks described are of approximately 3½ miles (5¾ km) and 5½ miles (8¾ km) long. The longer walk will take a minimum of 2 hours 20 minutes.

The walk could be subtitled "A tour of 17th Century Grade 2 listed buildings" - because you will pass a number. The timber framed Ye Olde Saracen's Head is one of them. The ancient route from this Inn to Temple Balsall, with its associations with the Knights Templar and the Knights Hospitallers, being called "The Knight's Way".

Opposite Ye Olde Saracen's Head, cross to the stile by the side of Elm Cottage and follow the fence round the side of the field to the stile at the bottom corner (a slight deviation from the Definitive Map route). Bear right to the stile to the left of the double electric pole. Having crossed the footbridge turn right and make for the gap between the end two bungalows. Follow the cul-de-sac round to the main road (white lines - Needlers End Lane) and turn left. After No 76 turn right up the track, along part of Speedwell Drive, in front of No. 4 and to the left of the MEB sub-station. At the next road (Station Road) turn right up to its junction with Balsall Street. Bear right to the field gate opposite. Go through the gate, after the stile, follow the hedge on the left to another stile and then turn right down the track past the farm buildings.

At the field, continue straight ahead to the stile and follow the hedge (on the right) to another stile in the corner which leads into the adjacent field. Follow the hedge on the left to the stile and then bear right to the footbridge. Cross the field to the stile and then cross the next field to the hedge corner - the hedge goes up the hill to between the farm buildings on the skyline and the path follows this hedge. At the top of the hill is a gate and from there we bear right along the track to Fen End Road (NB the track to the left is private).

From Fen End Road the shorter route is to the right (and is continued at the end of the text) and the longer route is to the left. After the white timber framed cottage, Woodside, cross the stile on the right. The next stile can be seen in the hedge beyond. From there cross to the hedge corner and follow the hedge (on the right) to the drive to Fen End Farm. Turn left along the drive and then right to the front of Moat Barn House, beyond which can be seen the next stile. Follow the hedge (on the right) round to the stile at the corner of the battery houses. Cross the footbridge and up the slope to continue at the back of the battery houses to the gate. Turn right along the track for a short distance to the stile on the left - then cross the narrow field to the gate by the

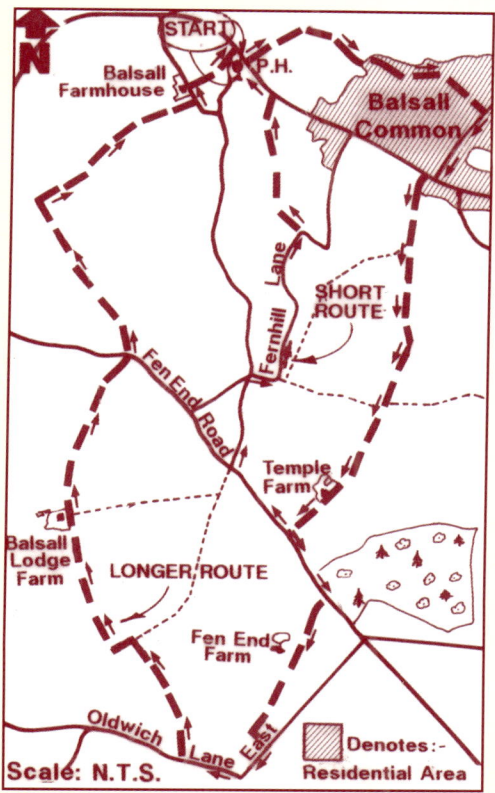

house. Turn left along the drive to the main road (Oldwych Lane East). Turn right along that road until just after Wroxall Cottages (opposite Hill Top Close), where the stile on the right is crossed and The Heart of England Way is followed - to the end of the walk.

After crossing this stile follow the fence, then cross to the gate which leads into the adjacent field. Turn left and follow the hedge on the left, until the farthest point of the third field. Turn left here over an unusually high stile - follow the hedge and turn right behind the old oak tree. Follow the hedge on the right until a small signpost directs you into a wooded area for a short distance. This deviation takes you into another field where the hedge is now on the left. At the hedge corner follow the path across two fields to the right of the wooded area around the farm. Continue along this track from Balsall Lodge Farm to Fen End Road. Turn right here and on the opposite side of the road, at the signpost, go down a narrow leafy path, with the boundary fence of Barracks Cottage on the left - this brings you out into a field. Follow the field edge path through this field and the next two, keeping the hedge on the right. At this third field corner, four hedges and four footpaths meet.

Turn right following the hedge towards the pylon. At the field corner, continue into the next field and follow the hedge (partly removed) on the right to the next stile. Bear left across a narrow field to the footbridge. From here cross the field to the edge of the copse which is to the left of the black and white timber framed Magpie Farmhouse. Go round the copse (a slight deviation here from the Definitive Map) to Magpie Lane. Turn left down the lane for some 80 paces and turn right into the field at the signpost. Follow, first the hedge and then the fence to gain access onto Magpie Lane at the side of the white house. Turn left back to the start point.

FOR THE SHORTER ROUTE: At Fen End Road, turn right for about 415 yards (380 metres). Turn right down Longbrook Lane and at the crossroads turn right along Fernhill Lane. At the bend beside the entrance to Howlett's Farm - go up the drive for a short distance and through the gate on the right. Turn left and follow the hedge to the corner where there is a gap in the hedge/fence in front. Cross the field to the hedge corner and follow the hedge (on the right) beyond to Balsall Street. Turn left back to the start point.

Extensions to this walk can be made with walks 7 and 9 in this booklet and walk 5 in booklet 1.

Castle Bromwich Hall

Castle Bromwich
Festival Way 1994

This walk is not a Country Walk since it is situated within Castle Bromwich Parish which is an almost totally built-up area. It was set out by the local Ramblers Association Group to celebrate 100 years of Castle Bromwich Parish Council. The inaugural walk was led by Frank Mackey, Chairman of the local group, as part of the Festival Week in March 1994.

The circular walk of approximately 5 miles (3km) starts from Arden Hall in Water Orton Road (GR4154 2899), where car parking is available and is mostly over off-road paths within the Parish. It also takes in three of the Council's areas of open space: The Ridge, Lanchester Park and Beechcroft Open Space. Adjacent to the route are a number of hostelries where refreshment can be taken and Castle Bromwich Gardens can also be visited. Look out for the distinctive Festival Way waymarkers at strategic points along the walk, on what is a fairly straightforward route. Toilet facilities are available adjacent to the playing fields at the back of Arden Hall. "Bromwich" means the village on the heath - "Castle" was a medieval addition which refers to the ancient Castle Mound situated to the north of Castle Bromwich Hall.

THE ROUTE: From Arden Hall turn left for a short distance along Water Orton Road, gaining access into Farthing Wood through the gap in the hedge at the end of the closeboard fence, just beyond the bus shelter. This wood is a remnant of the Forest of Arden. The local Ramblers Association with the help of the local infants school have planted woodland flowers, bulbs and erected bird boxes. The path through the various sections of this narrow wood ends at Hurst Lane North. Continue straight ahead along

Green Lane which becomes Auckland Drive. At Windward Way take the subway to Ribble Walk, which after Kingfisher Drive becomes Redwing Walk. Cross Auckland Drive into the grassed area of The Ridge - from here to the Castle Bromwich Hall Gardens is also part of A Solihull Way. Go up the bank, turn left and follow this grassed bank - cross the access road to the Collector Road into Bosworth's Wood and Lanchester Park. Continue through this park - after passing Lanchester School turn right along the footpath past Park Hall School to Water Orton Road. Cross the road, turn right and at the end of the housing, turn left into Beechcroft Open Space - see also Strolling in Solihull's Public Parks leaflet No.6.

Follow the paths through this Park and cross over Parkfield Drive. Just up the hill on this road is The Spitfire Public House - the name evokes memories of the wartime fighter plane which was built at the nearby factory at the former Castle Bromwich Airfield. The wartime experiences of the Chief Test Pilot, Alex Henshaw, can be read in his book "Sigh for a Merlin". Continue through the grassed area between housing and Collector Road, past the play area and continuing on the tarmac path which leads to Kingsleigh Drive. Go up Kyter Lane and then turn right up the unadopted Rectory Lane passing the Grade 2 listed buildings - Nos 1, 2 and 3 Rectory Lane. At the road junction at the top of the lane, turn right. After the Church turn left into the parkland, past the entrance to Castle Bromwich Hall Gardens. Continue round Castle Bromwich Hall to gain access onto Birmingham Road. Turn left and follow this road, past the front of Castle Bromwich Hall, after the mini-roundabout it becomes Chester Road (straight ahead) and then Water Orton Road - back to the start.

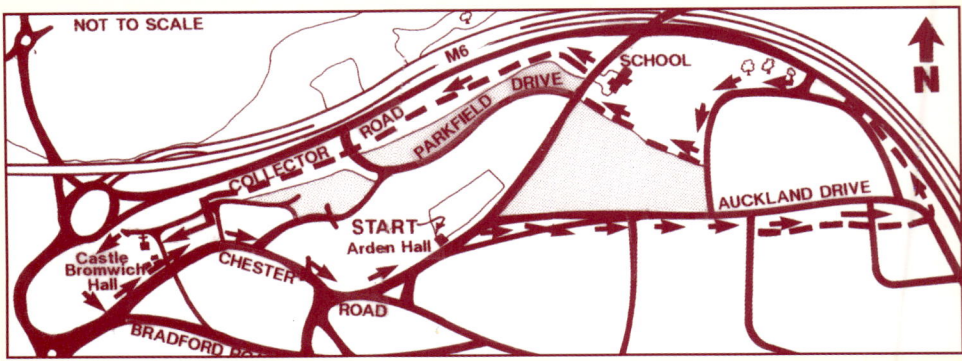

Places of Interest

Castle Bromwich Hall is a Jacobean style 17th Century mansion which is Grade 1 listed, as is the Bakehouse. The Stable Block and Pigeon House, both Grade 2 buildings, complete an interesting group. The Hall is now used as offices and is not open to the Public.

Castle Bromwich Hall Gardens: Restoration continues on what is regarded as the best surviving English formal garden of the period 1680-1730. Restoration commenced in 1985 with the formation of the Castle Bromwich Hall Gardens Trust. The gardens extend to eight acres and are open to the Public between Easter and the end of September between 1.30 and 4.30 on Mondays - Thursdays (inclusive) and between 2 and 6 on Saturdays, Sundays and Public Holidays.

The Church of St Mary and St Margaret is a 15th Century timber framed building which was entirely encased in red brick and stone in the 18th Century.

Meer End to Kenilworth Castle

6 miles

This is a circular walk from Table Oak Road, just off the A4177, at Meer End to historic Kenilworth Castle over public rights of way, initially in Solihull, but, mostly in Warwickshire. It is dedicated to the members of the Kenilworth Footpath Reservation Group who have adopted all the paths on the walk. Parking on the verge at Table Oak Road (GR 4244-2744) or with permission at the Tipperary Inn (or alternatively at Kenilworth Castle Brays Car Park GR 4281-2721).

The circular walk of 6 miles (9¾ km) will take a minimum of 2½ hours. This does not include any time taken to explore Kenilworth Castle and its environs.

The Tipperary Inn and nearby Tipperary Cottage acknowledge the connection between Harry Williams and Jack Judge who wrote the song "It's a long way to Tipperary" in 1912.

At the road junction turn right and follow the footpath opposite Tipperary Cottage. Initially the path is at right angles to the road, then it turns right keeping parallel with the road and crossing numerous drives and over many stiles. When the stile with the bridleway waymarkers (blue arrows) is reached, turn left. Poors Wood is on the right and then Black Hill Wood, on the left, is followed to its end. Turn right at the field following the wooded strip on the track. Turn left along the track towards Warriors Lodge Farm. Keep to the right of the silos and then right along the drive. At the wood, turn right down the track. At the gateway turn left to follow the fence parallel with the wood on the left, one field distant.

At the next stile and plankbridge we catch the first sight of the red sandstone towers of our objective. After crossing the track bear left through the remaining earthworks of The Pleasance (a large timber framed banqueting house used as state appartments, built by Henry V and demolished by Henry VIII) towards the waymarker post in front of the two oak trees. The narrow path becomes a track and in the dip before the houses in Kenilworth is the stile on the left (A) where we turn back - unless you want to have a closer look at the Castle.

Before the thatched cottage turn right to go round the Castle ramparts. Kenilworth Castle is an English Heritage site open every day except 24-26 December. Late March - End October 10-6 and 1 November - Late March 10-4.

From A, bear left. At the first stile take the left-hand path. Before dropping down to the second stile - look back to take in a superb view of the Castle. Keep on the same line to the field corner and then follow the hedge on the right to the stile. Cross the field to the stile and beyond towards the right-hand house. At the road turn right and almost immediately cross the stile. Follow the hedge on the left and then turn left before the pond. At the next pond cross over two fields. At the hedge turn left. After the pond turn right to follow the hedge on the right to the gateway where we turn left under the pylon. Look out for the waymarker post showing the route across the field towards the buildings. Continue round the boundary to turn left through the hedge after the refurbished outbuildings.

At the drive turn left and at the entrance gate to the impressive Rudfyn Manor, turn right to follow the fence to the stile at the field corner. Turn right and follow the hedge on the right to the gateway. Cross the field to the two stiles. Follow the hedge on the right - after the second gate the hedge is now on the left. At the stile with the dogway, by the riding stables, cross to the buildings (stile by two willows). Go round the side of the riding stables onto the drive and back to the Tipperary Inn.

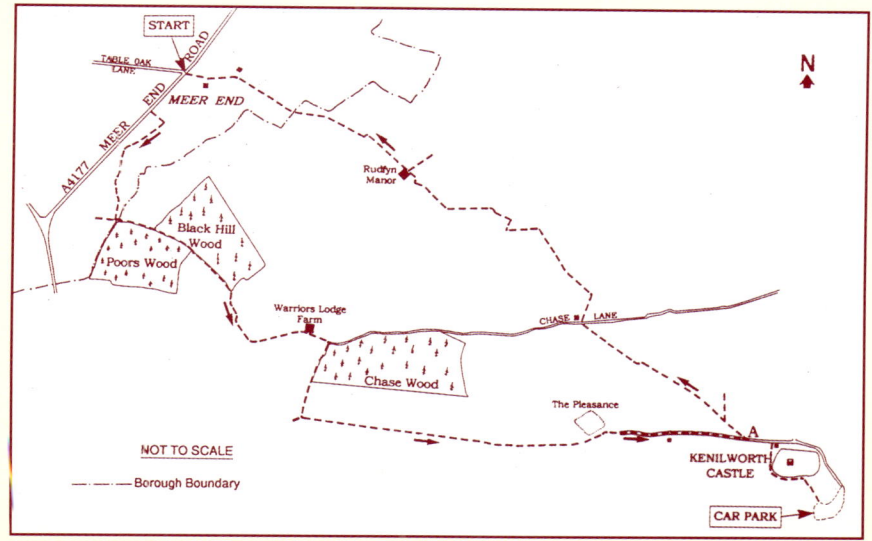

OTHER PUBLICATIONS

A SOLIHULL WAY *brochure and descriptive leaflets by Solihull MBC*

STROLLING IN SOLIHULL'S PUBLIC PARKS *10 free leaflets by Solihull MBC*

STROLL THROUGH KNOWLE *leaflet by Solihull MBC*

TWELVE COUNTRY WALKS IN SOLIHULL *by Solihull MBC*

A COVENTRY WAY *by Cyril J Bean*

A SHORT GUIDE TO CENTRAL KNOWLE *by The Knowle Society*

ELMDON HERITAGE WALK *(leaflet) by Friends of Elmdon*

FAVOURITE WALKS IN THE WEST MIDLANDS *by Members of Birmingham CHA Rambling Club*

THE HEART OF ENGLAND WAY *(5th Edition) by John Roberts*

MERIDEN WALKS *by John Smith*

NORTH WORCESTERSHIRE PATH WALKERS GUIDE *by Hereford and Worcester County Council*

PUB WALKS IN WARWICKSHIRE *by Richard Shurey*

TEN WALKS AROUND COVENTRY *by Coventry Ramblers Association*

THE GRAND UNION CANAL WALK *by Anthony Burton and Neil Curtis*

THE NAVIGATION WAY *by Peter Groves and Trevor Antill*

Useful Addresses and Contacts

SMBC ENVIRONMENT SERVICES DEPARTMENT
*PO Box 19
Council House
Solihull B91 3QT
Footpaths: Telephone 0121 704 6429 (George Kenneth)*

SMBC TOURIST INFORMATION CENTRE
*Central Library
Homer Road
Solihull B91 3RG
Telephone: 0121 704 6130/6134*

LOCAL BUS AND TRAIN TIMES
Centro 0121 200 2700

BRITISH HORSE SOCIETY
*Stoneleigh Deer Park
Kenilworth
Warwickshire CV8 2XZ*

BRITISH WATERWAYS
*Brome Hall Lane
Lapworth
Solihull
West Midlands B94 6LH*

BYWAYS AND BRIDLEWAYS TRUST
*St Mary's Business Centre,
Oystershell Lane,
Newcastle Upon Tyne
NE4 5QS*

COUNTRYSIDE COMMISSION
*John Dower House
Crescent Place
Cheltenham
Glos GL50 3RA*

HEART OF ENGLAND WAY ASSOCIATION
*John Watts
20 Throckmorton Road
Alcester
Warwickshire B49 6QA*

THE NATIONAL TRUST
*Severn Regional Office
Mythe End House
Tewkesbury
Glos GL20 6EB*

THE OPEN SPACES SOCIETY
*25A Bell Street
Henley on Thames
Oxon RG9 2BA*

THE RAMBLERS' ASSOCIATION
*1/5 Wandsworth Road
London SW8 2XX*

Follow the Country Code

- *Enjoy the Countryside and respect its life and work.*
- *Guard against all risk of fire.*
- *Fasten all gates.*
- *Keep your dogs under close control and on a lead when near farm animals. NB: Animals with young require special attention.*
- *Keep to the public paths across farmland.*
- *Use gates and stiles to cross fences, hedges and walls.*
- *Leave livestock, crops and machinery alone.*
- *Take your litter home.*
- *Help to keep all water clean.*
- *Protect wildlife, plants and trees.*
- *Take special care on country roads.*
- *Make no unnecessary noise.*